Effective Performance

Review Interviews

A self-help guide

KENNETH R ROBINSON

Institute of Personnel Management

Printed in Great Britain by
Latimer Trend & Company Ltd, Plymouth

British Library Cataloguing in Publication Data

Robinson, Kenneth R.
    Effective performance review interviews.
    1. Employment management—Performance standards.
    I. Title.
    658.3'1124   HF5549.5.P35
    ISBN 0-85292-327-9

Contents

Introduction

This booklet has been produced because performance review (PR) or appraisal interviewing appears to be an area of our jobs as managers which presents us with a certain amount of difficulty.[1] Sometimes senior management assumes that we already have the skill and knowledge required to carry out the task satisfactorily. In consequence we are not given the training or guidance we need. Often we are reluctant to conduct interviews because of lack of confidence in our own ability, a fear of being unable to cope with conflict, possibly resulting in loss of face and authority. Many of us also find it embarrassing to discuss personal performance with our employees and try to keep our true feelings about it to ourselves. In Douglas McGregor's words, we are not comfortable when 'put in the position of playing God'.[2]

It is important that we overcome such difficulties. In general they arise because of a lack of understanding of what is required of us. Set out in the following pages are some guidelines on conducting PR interviews competently. They are objective and should help to give greater self assurance in carrying out this aspect of our jobs, thus improving our own effectiveness as well as that of our employees.

Effective performance review interviews

What is performance review?

Performance review is a two-way process which enables us to assess the past and present performance of our employees, to agree future activity plans with them and to give help and guidance towards optimizing their capabilities to meet both corporate and personal goals.

The more detailed objectives of the system might be to:

obtain data for manpower planning, promotion, transfer, demotion, redundancy, dismissal, salary administration, career development, training, up-dating job descriptions

assess employee performance and motivate individuals to make the best of their capabilities by the use of achievable targets, feedback and review

improve communications generally

handle change whether brought about by the organization or by the individual

provide a record of personal assessments.

The need for a PR system is therefore irrefutable. Since organizational objectives can only be attained if individual employees carry out their designated functions adequately, it follows that we must monitor their efficiency continuously and provide every assistance to them to optimize their performance.

In most cases, if we have direct responsibility for the work of an employee, we are likely to be best fitted to carry out his PR interview. Since we are closest to the job, we should not only know what is entailed but should also be familiar with the employee's capabilities and idiosyncrasies. However, this must not be applied as a hard and fast rule. The circumstances of the relationship must be taken into account. If it does not work, it would be in no one's interest to prolong the struggle. If mutual respect and trust are lacking and it is seen that nothing can be done about it, another solution must be sought. The interviewer's immediate superior can often help in this event.

Sometimes it is found that a three-way interview (grandfather, father, son) is effective. It should be borne in mind, however, that some employees may feel outnumbered in this situation and therefore under greater pressure. It is important that the interviewee's feelings are taken into account. If they are not, we may not get the responses or the co-operation we expect.

Whatever method may be chosen for the interviews, they will have less than the desired impact if top management commitment is lacking. Indeed, the support of everyone at all levels in the organization is necessary for the corporate value of a PR scheme to be fully realized. All interviewers have a responsibility for encouraging this support.

What are the problems?

We have to avoid certain pitfalls if a PR system is to be successful. The following list is not in order of importance:

viewing PR as an unwelcome activity dictated by the system rather than part of our normal day to day responsibilities

lack of preparation and clearly understood objectives, so that we do not use interview time profitably

failure to link the objectives to the true needs of the organization[3]

a tendency to be subjective and use the wrong criteria for assessment. For example, we rely on personality and other factors not directly related to performance

assessment criteria, although commonly agreed throughout the organization, are not interpreted in the same way by everyone involved

we may not always be in touch with everything that is going on and may rely too much on what we are told by the interviewees or on how things may appear on the surface we may be reluctant to come to grips with problems which may be embarrassing to either party

if we adopt an autocratic style, one result may be that we create targets which the employee does not feel are achievable

the difficulties of measuring the effects of factors which prevent targets being met, particularly those outside the control of the employee

we make assumptions that because an employee is good or bad in one aspect of his job, he is equally good or bad in others. A similar groundless supposition may be, for example, that if he is like us he must be acceptable

where a continuous assessment system is not used, an isolated incident which occurs just prior to a review interview can influence our judgement out of all proportion to its importance

assessments may be more honest if they are not seen by the employee than if they are

linking salary review with performance review at the same interview may cause emotive responses[4]

lack of flexibility. Some of us depend too much on what the job description says and not enough on the reality of the situation

employees may feel at a disadvantage when being judged by the boss and may therefore be on the defensive.

Clearly these difficulties give us some clues as to what areas we should explore in order to establish a successful approach to performance reviews.

Procedure

As with most aspects of our jobs as managers, there is merit in adopting a systematic approach. One advantage is that an accepted method of operation helps to ensure consistency, so that everyone involved knows where he stands. Another benefit is that it gives us greater confidence in our ability to discharge this important responsibility effectively. The employees themselves also feel that they are getting a fair deal and are having a say in how their jobs should be carried out. We must be on our guard against allowing PR interviews to develop into a mechanistic activity, however, and should be constantly reviewing our procedures in the light of experience and change.

The procedure should be considered in three stages:

1 preparation
2 the review interview
3 follow up.

1 Preparation

This is a stage which is so often neglected, with unhappy consequences. If we do not have a fairly clear idea as to how we are going to conduct the interview, we may well find ourselves carried along by it and neglect issues which are important. We owe it to the employee concerned to give the matter a good deal of thought and to come to the interview fully prepared. Just playing it by ear is not good enough. The employee's whole career may depend on it and so might our own reputation in the long run.

The major factors to be considered in our preparation are:

objectives of the exercise
physical conditions in the interview room
time allocation
organizational policies, systems, procedures that may be relevant
data which will be needed
structure of the interview
the employee himself
possible outcomes.

Objectives

Many of our PR interviews are carried out without a clear understanding of what we are setting out to achieve. A broad definition of purpose has been given on page 2, but we need to be much more precise about our objectives in any given situation. For instance, whilst the majority of our interviews will concentrate on reviewing performance against previously agreed targets and deciding new targets for a forthcoming period, situations will arise which justify special consideration.

For example, there may be difficulties with an employee who always meets his targets but upsets everyone else in doing so. We do not necessarily want to carry out a disciplinary interview in this case, unless all else has failed, but will want to handle the problem through the normal PR channels. Planning in advance how we are going to manage this problem is important, since trying to deal with it in an *ad hoc* way may bring emotive responses and over reaction.

Another example may be that a supervisory job has arisen in our department and we have to tell one of our employees who was expecting to get it that he has been unsuccessful. Clearly we need to have worked out sound reasons for rejecting him and must be prepared to explain these to the employee if asked to do so. In some instances he will concede that another candidate is better suited to the position than he is and will not seek any further justification. In others, however, he may feel very strongly about his own suitability and we should be willing and able to discuss our decision freely with him.

These cases illustrate that no two interviews are alike and it is imperative that we should prepare our strategy carefully before we embark on them. New facts may emerge during the interview which call for tactical changes, but this prospect should not deter us from formulating clear objectives as we see them before the event.

Physical conditions in the interview room
Any interview situation requires the undivided attention of both parties. Wherever possible we should select a room which is comfortable and in which the dialogue can proceed without being overheard or interrupted. This means, amongst other things, that the physical conditions should not reflect the boss/subordinate relationship too strongly and interruptions from telephone calls or visitors should be prevented.

Time allocation
The dialogue should be open and relaxed. We therefore need to choose the time at which it starts with care and allocate an adequate period of time to it. Neither interviewer nor interviewee should feel that he is under undue pressure. If we cannot be reasonably certain that the required amount of time is available, it would be better for us to postpone the interview until we can. Both parties should know in advance what time is being set aside and how it will be used.

Organizational factors
The subject of every interview will be affected in some way by organizational factors. Policies, systems, procedures arising at corporate or departmental level will influence the conditions under which we operate. These therefore have to be examined carefully where relevant to the specific situation.

6

For example, we may have to deal with an employee who is a few years from retirement and is anxious about his future with the organization. We should not attempt to carry out such an interview without ensuring that we know precisely what the organization's retirement policy is.

The relevant information on organizational factors and any constraints imposed by them must therefore be obtained before the interview. Except where totally unexpected circumstances arise, we should not have to interrupt or adjourn interviews in order to acquaint ourselves with the required facts.

Data required

Clearly, adequate preparation for an interview requires the collection of all the appropriate facts of the case. We must remind ourselves of the targets previously agreed and must refer to any interim notes we may have made on the employee's performance. Influences on his success or failure in meeting those targets must be assessed. Some of these factors will be within his control, some outside it. We must be careful to distinguish between them. It may be that some will not come to light until the interview. We should be sufficiently familiar with the detail of the employee's work to be able to consider in advance what his targets should be for the ensuing period, always bearing in mind that these could be modified in the light of new information.

In a sense, the whole of the period since the last review is one of preparation for the current one. It is strongly recommended that we do not depend entirely upon these interviews to review our employees' performance. This should be assessed on a continuous basis. The work of our department should be monitored in such a way that deviations from its objectives may be dealt with promptly as the unplanned circumstances arise. Leaving things until the next review may waste a good deal of valuable time.

Structure of the interview

The interview should be structured in such a way that the matters discussed may be dealt with in the most efficient way possible. Conducting interviews in a casual and random manner gives rise to inefficiencies due to back-tracking, diversions, exclusions, over- or under-emphasis and so on. We need to channel our energies so as to make the best use of the time available and both interviewer and interviewee should know what to expect. In the interests of consistency, a framework should be agreed which will be much the same for all review meetings. It is important, however, that we maintain some flexibility in our approach and are not hampered in discussing important issues by a rigid, mechanistic routine. The style we adopt will of course vary with the interviewee and the relationship that normally exists between us.

A suggested, though not inflexible, framework for a review meeting is:

outline the purpose of the meeting

ask the employee to report and comment on the last period's work

refer to targets previously agreed and give assessment of performance against these targets

discuss any shortfalls in performance and agree action by either or both parties as required

agree targets for ensuing period, including any training that may be considered necessary

check understanding, record agreements and sign relevant documents

inform anyone else who may be involved.

The employee

Paying due regard to the needs of the employee is important.[5] We should remember that, whatever may be in our own minds about the way in which the interview will be conducted, the employee will not be privy to it. He may have some misgivings about the possible outcome and how it may affect his future. If we normally adopt an open management style in the day to day conduct of our affairs, this may be less of a problem, but the employee will always have underlying apprehensions for which we must make allowance.

PR systems, when first introduced, can generate a good deal of suspicion and often outright hostility. They should therefore be embarked upon with the utmost care and sensitivity to the feelings of the employees. Much of their concern will be due to fear of change and so the benefits to them of introducing such a system need to be explained fully. Once they can be convinced that the motives are in the best interests of everyone, they will accept performance reviews as something which makes an important contribution to business performance through, among other things, improved management-employee relations.

One way in which the employee can be helped to come to terms with the review interview is to ensure that he is always given adequate time in which to prepare for it. It is just as important for him as for us to give prior consideration to the review. Calling him into the office without notice and then informing him that 'This is a PR interview' is unpardonable and is most unlikely to bring the desired responses. Indeed, it will stand a good chance of building up antipathy which is counter productive, precisely the reverse effect to the one we are seeking.

We must prepare ourselves for possible reactions to what we have to say and try to decide in advance how we can respond to them. It is too easy to react unfavourably when we get an unexpected answer from an employee in a discussion. We may be tempted into making instant judgements which are totally wrong.

The importance of continuous performance monitoring has been mentioned. The penalty for merely conducting interviews at six or twelve monthly intervals could be serious. If an employee has made an unfortunate error or had some kind of lapse just prior to the interview so that the circumstances are still fresh in our minds, we might be unduly influenced by this, even though his performance in the rest of the review period was perfectly acceptable. 'Critical incident' can operate in the reverse direction as well. Knowing that a review is imminent, an employee may assume a high profile in the hope of influencing the outcome in his favour. If we keep notes of our employees' performances on a continuing basis, we may avoid falling into the trap of having our judgement coloured by such circumstances.

Possible outcomes

We should never sit back and assume that the outcome of a review will always be as we planned it. We must cater for any eventuality. When targets are met satisfactorily there is no problem. When the employee fails to meet them, however, the cause must be identified and the effects measured. The reasons may have been outside his control though not necessarily outside our sphere of influence. For example, he may have been prevented from carrying out his responsibilities because of lack of co-operation from another employee or department. We then need to take direct action ourselves to deal with the problem and to see that this situation does not arise again.

Where the failures are within the employee's control, we need to ask ourselves whether they arise from his lack of knowledge or skills or by reason of his own negligence. In any of these circumstances, he may require training, so we should know what training solutions are available to us. We should also be aware of the possible effects of taking the wrong training action. For instance, training which was arranged at the last review may have failed to have the desired effect or may even have

9

exceeded our intentions. In the latter case, the employee may now feel better qualified for promotion, may no longer be content with his present job and may therefore fail to perform satisfactorily through lack of interest and application. Another outcome may be the discovery that the employee has reached the limit of his ability and is found to be in the wrong job. These situations cannot be ignored and must be dealt with as a matter of urgency.

When a need for further training for an employee is identified, we are inclined to ask the personnel and/or training department to take the necessary action with the minimum of information. We have a responsibility to discuss with that department our answers to a number of questions which are listed in the appendix on page 18. Armed with these facts they should be better equipped to arrange training which is appropriate to the established need. The practice of arbitrarily selecting a packaged course which looks vaguely useful is to be deprecated.

There is a tendency for training in the PR process itself to be confined to the administrators of the overall scheme and the interviewers. Since the basis of a review interview is a two-way contract between employer and employee, it follows that the latter should have the same opportunity for training in the process as the former.

Another possible outcome of a PR interview is the bringing to light of facts which may promote some form of disciplinary action, due for example to an employee's negligence. In this event, the case would be taken out of the PR process and the organization's disciplinary procedure invoked. Guidance in handling matters of this kind is given in the ACAS Code of Practice.[6]

2 The review interview

The review interview itself requires consideration of a number of factors which have been summarized under the following headings:

the right climate
employee's own assessment
interviewer's assessment
targetting and training for results
interpreting employee behaviour
assessment methods and criteria
response to change
handling difficult situations

disputes over targets
obligations on both sides
recording agreements.

The right climate

It is essential that the interview be conducted with tact, diplomacy and sensitivity. Creating the right climate at an early stage paves the way for a realistic and objective examination of an employee's performance with the benefit of his co-operation. He should see the meeting as a contract through which joint assessments are arrived at and joint decisions taken, and not merely as an opportunity for someone in authority to pass judgement on him. If targets are agreed rather than dictated, there is less risk of a misunderstanding leading to wasted time and effort.

Both parties should understand clearly the purpose of the interview. Preparing for the wrong agenda is not only inefficient but highly frustrating for the other person whose subsequent reaction may be less than helpful. No one attending a meeting should have to make assumptions about what is going to be discussed. In general it is better to separate salary review from other performance reviews although some of the data obtained in the latter will inevitably be used in the former.

Employee's own assessment

We should give the employee the first opportunity to comment on how he sees his own achievements and failures over the period being examined. When we do not agree with what he has to say, the temptation to interrupt him should be resisted. Instead, we should hear him out, making *brief* notes for further reference if required. If we occupy ourselves with detailed scribblings whilst he is talking, this is likely to be unnerving for him and may distract him as he tries to read what we are writing. We should concentrate on what he is saying and not what we might want to say ourselves. We should also try not to make subjective judgements based on factors which do not contribute directly to his performance and therefore cannot be measured in performance terms.

Interviewer's assessment

Having heard the employee's self appraisal, we can now refer him to the targets agreed at the last review and state our own assessment of his performance. Where there is agreement that the targets have been met, it may be appropriate to offer some encouragement in the form of praise for a job well done. Where shortfalls are evident, the nature and extent of these should be agreed between the two parties before any attempt is made to take remedial steps. Without trying to apportion blame, we must establish to what extent the employee could have influenced his results. Suitable action can then be agreed to rectify any omissions and to prevent recurrence of similar unsatisfactory performance in the future (*see* 'Possible outcomes' on page 9). In extreme circumstances, such as gross negligence, the matter has to be taken outside the PR process as previously mentioned. Indeed, such shortcomings may have become apparent before the regular review and may have been dealt with separately. In this event, provided further disciplinary measures are not necessary, we would follow up the initial action with suitable counselling at the PR interview.[7]

Targetting and training for results

Targetting is of course at the centre of the PR system. An employee's work performance can be assessed adequately only if it can be measured against specific work targets which are achievable. If this cannot be done the assessment will be incomplete or the judgement made on the wrong criteria, eg personality factors. We must decide precisely what work we expect him to do, the standard required and the time scale, all of which must be recorded and agreed. It is not sufficient for us to tell a craftsman to make as many units as he can in the specified time. Not only must we tell him how many units he has to achieve in the appropriate period but also make it clear what quality standards, eg tolerances and reject/scrap limits, must be met. In this way, what is required and what is achieved can be more readily compared.[8]

Sometimes the failure to meet targets will point to a deficiency in the employee's training in certain aspects of his job. Once the precise requirements are identified, a suitable training programme to deal with them will become one of the employee's targets for the ensuing period. Care must be taken not to consider an employee's performance in isolation. His work does, of course, have an impact on many other activities outside his department. Since his contribution to overall business performance is the parameter to be measured, it is important that its effects on these activities are taken into account when assessing his work. It can hardly be regarded as in the organization's interests if in satisfying his departmental objectives he causes chaos elsewhere in the business.

Direct accusations could exacerbate the problem of the employee not meeting his targets, because he will feel that we are only interested in attributing blame. Tactful questioning is therefore necessary, the underlying theme being that we are trying to help the employee to solve his problems and realize his potential. The removal of threats often provides the key to the discussion of his difficulties in an atmosphere of honesty and frankness. The issues may have to be pursued in some depth and the value of indirect and non-leading questions should not be ignored in achieving this.[9]

Interpreting employee behaviour
In every interviewing situation it is necessary to be able to interpret the behaviour of the interviewee. His response or lack of response to questions will often reflect his feelings, not only about his work environment but also about his life outside the job, which can sometimes be quite complex. His motivation to work and to be a useful member of society will depend upon factors which bring him satisfaction or result in dissatisfaction. Much has been written about human behaviour in organizations. The research findings on motivation are well summarized by John Hunt in his book *Managing people at work*.[10]

In some circumstances, where it is difficult to elicit information from the employee because he simply finds revealing some of the facts embarrassing, we may have to adopt a more positive line of questioning. It may be necessary for us to probe these areas, because we have a right to know and a duty to find out what factors are preventing the employee from performing. Nevertheless, this can be done with discretion and it is worthwhile adopting an empathetic approach. In other words, we should ask ourselves what kind of questions we would respond to favourably if we were in the other person's shoes.

Assessment methods and criteria
Throughout the interview we should ensure that both parties understand what is being said. Jargon and ambiguous language can lead to serious communications problems. These can also arise within the PR system itself. If the organization sets criteria against which employees are to be assessed, the interpretation of these criteria must be clear and consistent. The assessment methods used vary considerably between organizations.[11] As they are written up in detail elsewhere, only brief mention will be made of them here. Many of the traditional methods, which can be somewhat mechanistic, are still used and include ranking, alphabetical and numerical rating, personality trait rating, forced choice rating and written reports. They tend to highlight our human weaknesses in making

judgements about other people. We are too easily diverted from an objective approach by instinctive consideration of factors such as personality which may not have any direct bearing on performance. In other words, whatever criteria are used there is a real risk that they will be applied inconsistently and subjective considerations will take over.

A method used for management and supervisory personnel is the assessment centre.[12] This makes use of group techniques to assess potential and involves a team of highly qualified assessors observing the employee's performance in a variety of individual and group activities such as tests and management games over a number of days. Since assessment centres demand a high level of expertise from the assessors and a substantial period of time away from the job for the managers, they are very costly.[13] Nonetheless, they have their place in assessing managerial performance and future potential.[14]

Whatever method we choose for performance reviews, it is desirable that it is results orientated since results are what we are seeking from all our employees. Thus the system, wherever possible, should provide for clearly defined targets and a ready measure of achievement or non achievement. One method using this approach is management by objectives (MBO).[15] Although not completely free of criticism, in that *inter alia* subjectivity cannot be entirely avoided, it goes a long way towards offering an effective PR philosophy. As with all management techniques, it requires commitment and responsibility at all levels to be successful.

Response to change
When carrying out PR interviews it is important that we do not depend rigidly on what the employee's job description says about his work. Reality may be very different and we should make allowances for that. We and our employees must respond to change and progress. On occasions the interviewee will bring to light some entirely new information which needs to be investigated before the review can proceed. In these circumstances, the meeting should be adjourned for a specified time to allow the necessary examination to be made.

Handling difficult situations
How do we deal with the interview which goes badly? With all the good will in the world on our part there will be times when clashes will occur. Before attempting to solve the problem we need to ascertain what it is. The employee may be tense and unco-operative for a whole variety of

reasons and it brings a solution much nearer to find out exactly what is troubling him. Prevention is better than cure of course and the creation of a climate of trust in our regular dealings with the employee will help to remove antagonism. Furthermore, if in the interview the employee is encouraged to give his own assessment of what has happened initially, as suggested earlier, there is less chance of his being able to build up strong feelings against us. Where we are dissatisfied with his performance and make the error of showing our hand first, he may come under attack from us without his case, if he has one, being heard at all. If things become really difficult, even violent, it is vitally necessary that we keep calm. When violence in an interview elicits no reaction from us, it does not achieve its ends and sooner or later it has to be abandoned. It is worth remembering that it takes two people to have a slanging match. Where all else fails, the heat must be taken out of the situation by an adjournment. The way in which this is proposed to the interviewee is critical. He must not be made to feel that he is solely to blame for the lack of rapport.

Disputes over targets

Disputes about whether or not targets have been met arise mainly because there was something wrong with them in the first place. If care is not taken over the wording of targets, a loophole is provided for the employee to question their meaning when he has not performed satisfactorily, even though he agreed to them in the first place. When we have taken precautions to word the targets unambiguously, the only problem that remains is agreeing on what factors prevented the employee from meeting the requirements and which of these were within his control. These are usually matters of fact, not just opinion.

When targets are being discussed for the ensuing period we may find that the interviewee disputes that they are achievable. One reason for this is that he may want to build some slack into the system so that he does not have to work at too high a pressure. Another may be that he has no confidence that the resources necessary for him to carry out his part of the task will be forthcoming. He needs to be reassured on these matters. When he genuinely feels that he cannot achieve the suggested targets, it is no more reassuring to him to say 'Of course you can' than to say to a natural worrier 'Don't worry.' We must provide evidence to show that a similar situation in the past was satisfactorily handled by him within the agreed time scale. We must also satisfy ourselves that the targets really are attainable by that particular employee. Different people have widely differing thresholds of pressure and responsibility.

Obligations on both sides

It has been mentioned that performance review should be seen as a contract between the two parties. This means that both parties have obligations and we should make sure that we have followed up our part of any previous agreements made. What we ourselves have done should be communicated to the employee at an early stage of the interview. If we have failed to carry out any of our promises we may put the contract under a certain amount of strain.

Recording agreements

Before the interview is closed, it is important to record unambiguously what has been agreed between the parties, otherwise the arguments which may arise could result in valuable time being lost during the ensuing period. It is a good idea to make sure that both parties sign the appropriate document to confirm their agreement.

3 Follow up

It is easy to go away from a PR interview and forget the action that has been agreed. Clearly the follow up of such decisions is a vital stage in the whole procedure and both parties must see to it that they comply with the agreements as soon as they can reasonably do so. This may require diary entries and setting aside a certain amount of time to deal with all the relevant points.

We would also be wise to regard performance review not as a once or twice yearly activity but a continuous one. If we confer with our employees and keep notes on their performance on a fairly regular basis throughout the review period, we not only avoid the 'critical incident' phenomenon but also build up a more co-operative relationship with them. It is a worthwhile procedure for us to review our own handling of the PR interview soon after the event. There are always lessons to be learned from considering whether or not we were satisfied with the way in which we handled the activity. If we feel that our own performance in the interview needs revision, we should record this for future reference and take suitable remedial action.

Conclusion

Performance review need not be the scourge that many managers consider it to be. If we are to be judged on our results, we owe it to ourselves as well as to the organization to get the best contributions from our employees. Performance review goes a long way towards achieving this objective if we use the technique skilfully.

The success of performance review depends very much on the rapport that is set up between ourselves and the interviewee. If the day to day relationship already existing between us is one of active co-operation, performance review merely becomes a formalization of our regular dialogue. If not, the benefits of our adopting a more democratic management style could be given serious consideration. Not only might this be in the best interests of the organization but we may well make our own task easier.

Although performance review clearly sets out to systematize the activities of employees, it does not have to be mechanical. What is important is that everyone knows what results are expected of him and his performance can be measured against the targets agreed between him and the manager responsible. Circumstances do arise where employees fail to meet their targets and the sooner we identify these problems and deal with them the better. A sound performance review system can improve employee morale, because people are involved in the setting of their own targets, the likelihood of time being wasted in pursuing unclear objectives is minimized and the employees as well as the organization can benefit from more efficient performance.

There must, of course, be commitment on both sides. The task is not completed when we set our employee to work again after a performance review interview. We have to monitor the situation continuously and take action without delay as and when it becomes necessary. It is also vital that any personal undertakings we may give an employee at an interview are fulfilled at the earliest opportunity. Obtaining commitment from the employee should not be so difficult if we create a climate of openness and trust. Suspicion of the management's motives and lack of adequate information are probably the greatest deterrents to getting the job done satisfactorily.

Appendix: training checklist

If a training need has been identified from a PR interview, the following questions need to be answered at various stages of the training process:

(i) can the requirements be met without using a formal training course, eg by:

> individual coaching
> prescribed reading
> programmed learning
> project work
> job rotation
> job assignments
> reallocation of duties within the department
> further education course?

(ii) are both you and your employee agreed as to what needs to be done?

(iii) do you see this training as part of your employee's development within the organization, not just a shot in the arm to deal with one situation?

(iv) what objectives do you expect the training to meet, eg:

> introduction to a job or function
> basic understanding of a job or function
> provision of skills to carry out a job or function
> developing technical knowledge within a specialized field
> broadening knowledge of the business or organization as a whole
> changing attitudes about the job, function or organization?

(v) will the proposed training meet the needs of the organization?

(vi) will it meet your objectives and those of the employee?

(vii) will the content of the programme be suitable in depth and scope?

(viii) will the programme methods be conducive to your employee's learning, eg:

> direct teaching
> self instruction
> participative
> a balanced mix?

(ix) where other learners are involved, will the mix of participants be helpful or a hindrance to your employee's learning?

(x) do you have any preferences as to:

> the length of the programme
> where it should take place
> whether residential or not
> whether full or part time
> the costs involved?

(xi) have you briefed your employee for the training, in particular in relation to:

> why he is undertaking it
> what he will be expected to learn
> how he will be able to apply the knowledge gained?

(xii) has he been given any help he may need to prepare himself for the training programme, eg by re-organizing his work?

(xiii) have you paved the way for him to use his new knowledge when he returns, eg by departmental or job changes?

(xiv) after the training, have you de-briefed him to ascertain:

> what learning took place
> how it will be used in the job
> what were his feelings about the content and the quality of the training?

(xv) have you obtained a written report from him?

(xvi) have the findings of his report been communicated to those who need to know?

(xvii) have you drawn up an action plan to make optimum use of your employee's new learning and to remove any obstacles to his future effective performance?

References

1 ROWE Kay H. An appraisal of appraisals. *Journal of Management Studies*. Vol 1, No 1, March 1964. pp 1–25

2 MCGREGOR Douglas M. An uneasy look at performance appraisal. *Harvard Business Review*. Vol 35, No 3, May–June 1957. pp 89–94

3 SAVAGE Adrian. Reconciling your appraisal system with company reality. *Personnel Management*. Vol 14, No 5, May 1982. pp 31–33

4 ANSTEY Edgar, FLETCHER Clive A. *and* WALKER James. *Staff appraisal and development*. London, Allen and Unwin, 1976

5 ROBINSON Kenneth R. *A practical approach to employee motivation*. Cambridge, Cambridge Management Training 1984

6 ACAS. DISCIPLINARY PRACTICE AND PROCEDURES IN EMPLOYMENT. Code of Practice No 1. HMSO, 1977

7 BOARD Robert de. *Counselling people at work: an introduction for managers*. Aldershot, Gower Publishing 1983

8 ROBINSON Kenneth R. *A handbook of training management*. London, Kogan Page Ltd, 1981. pp 164–66

9 JOHNSON Robert G. The appraisal interview guide. AMACOM, 1979
STEWART Valerie *and* STEWART Andrew. *Practical performance appraisal*. Farnborough, Gower Publishing 1977
RANDALL C. G. *et al. Staff Appraisal* 3rd edition. London, Institute of Personnel Management 1984

10 HUNT John W. *Managing people at work*. Maidenhead, McGraw Hill, 1979

11 GILL Deirdre. *Appraising performance—present trends and the next decade*. Institute of Personnel Management, 1977
ARMSTRONG Michael. *A handbook of personnel management practice*. 2nd edition. London, Kogan Page Ltd 1984. pp 161–169

12 STEWART Andrew. *The identification of management potential*. Institute of Manpower Studies, University of Sussex, 1971

13 UNGERSON Bernard. Assessment centres—a review of research findings. *Personnel Review*. Vol 3, No 3, Summer 1974
STEWART Andrew *and* STEWART Valerie. *Tomorrow's Managers Today*. London, Institute of Personnel Management, 1981. p 62 *et seq*

14 DULEWICZ Victor. The application of assessment centres. *Personnel Management*. Vol 14, No 9, September 1982. pp 32–35

15 MCGREGOR Douglas. *The human side of enterprise*. New York, McGraw Hill, 1960
MORRISEY George. *Management by objectives and results for business and industry*. Reading, Mass., Addison Wesley 1977